Rest Awhile

By

VANCE HAVNER

Author of "Consider Him" "Road to Revival" "The Secret of Christian Joy" and "By the Still Waters" and more

www.solidchristianbooks.com

Contents

FOREWORD 4
1 HOME AGAIN 5
2 WHITTLING 7
3 COUNTRY PREACHING 9
4 A FRIEND OF GOD 11
5 PICKANINNY 14
6 IF YOU ARE NERVOUS 16
7 THIS WAY OUT 18
8 WHAT TO DO 21
9 "LET HIM ASK IN FAITH" 23
10 "I BELIEVE GOD" 25
11 PARTING 28
12 A STROLLER IN SNOW 30
13 WAKE UP! 33
14 THREE D'S 36
15 "A WAY OUT OF NO WAY" 39
16 "NOT SO, LORD" 41
17 ANOTHER CHANCE 44
18 PAULS PERSUASION 47
19 "BLESSED DOWNCASTINGS" 49
20 SPRING NOTES 51
21 MY CROWD 54
22 BELIEVE—DON'T STUDY ABOUT IT! 57
23 A LETTER TO DAD 59
24 OVERDOING AND UNDERDOING 61
25 THE TWO "SUFFICIENTS" 64

26 THE ETIQUETTE OF LOVE 66
27 FIGHTING THE STARS 68
28 "GOOD FOR NOTHING" 70
29 WHAT LACK I YET 72
30 GOING HOME 74

FOREWORD

EVER since I wrote *By the Still Waters,* while a country pastor, I have longed to write more in the same vein. Friends who say they were blessed by those rustic sketches have encouraged me to write a companion volume, but a city pastorate of five years and many preaching journeys over the land have not provided a suitable setting for rural reflections. One cannot write of these things in a hotel room.

It has become possible through circumstances, evidently the Lord's leading, to spend a few autumn weeks in the old home in the hills. No sooner had this opportunity opened before me than I felt impressed to return to my first love and resume the trail of reflections I left in the Carolina lowlands. Then it was the low country, and now it is the hills, but both are Carolina and both are "countrified" and I trust the theme in both cases is common to hearts everywhere.

A few of these sketches were published with some changes in the Charlotte (N. C.) *Observer,* and grateful acknowledgement is hereby made for permission to reprint them. But all of them are FOREWORD

A skin, and in these simple matters that abide time makes little difference. They are sent forth to the glory of our Lord Who spoke the colorful language of the outdoors and Who bade His disciples of old, "Come ye yourselves apart and rest awhile."

V. H.

Greensboro, N. C.

1 HOME AGAIN

I'M home again—and in October!

No combination of earthly joys could be finer. No place is sweeter, after months in the whirl of this insane world, than the house on the hill and the familiar paths in the woods, the simple sights and sounds back home. And though the poet asks, "What is so rare as a day in June?" we still hold out for October.

It may be that in autumn "the melancholy days have come, the saddest of the year," but there is balm and healing in the very tang of the air and one gathers fresh courage for whatever these days of world distress may bring as he watches the passing year gaily dress itself in the Joseph's coat of autumn to meet the white old age of winter. Would that we mortals might learn to fare forth as colorfully to meet whatever bleakness may lie ahead, knowing that beyond every winter lies always spring! And why should tide and season make any difference anyway, for "when I am happy in Him December's as pleasant as May"?

So here I am in the hills watching Autumn weave from the loom of Summer her robe of many colors. There is something subdued, serene, sublime about it all, something as good for our souls as the vitality of spring and the contentment of summer. "The frost is on the punkin and the fodder's in the shock." The woods are full of busy squirrels keyed up by the winey autumn air. It is 'possum-hunting time and com-shucking season, and there's brand new molasses for breakfast in the morning. Falling acorns tap the roof at night, and falling leaves somehow always carry a tinge of sadness and remind us of Byron's lament about his days being in the yellow leaf. But, thank God, when we know the Lord, the worm, the canker and the grief are not ours!

The only parachute troops out here are the dandelion aeronauts floating in the breeze, but they are out for life and not for death. The muscadines and scuppernongs are ripe and there is an elixir in their wild juice that all the drug stores cannot match. The persimmons are ready, too, and he who has not tasted real persimmon pudding fresh on the farm is simply one of the underprivileged, "in castles and palaces though he may roam."

Somehow, a lot of things don't matter when one comes back home. Back from this modern mad masquerade, where everybody lives in a strain trying to make everybody else think he is what he isn't, it is a relief to drop into plain, simple living where the journey of life is not spoiled by the baggage. I believe it was Josh Billings who said, "I'd rather know a few things for certain than be sure of a lot of things that ain't so." Somehow, the "few things for certain" seem more certain out here in the hills.

It's a perfect morning. Not a cloud in the sky. The haze of autumn rests lightly everywhere. There is a tonic in the air. I must stroll down the pasture lane and by the creek and through the woods and over the hills, away from cars and radios and all the noisy trappings of this progress that doesn't progress! It is good to get away from it all now and then, for we cannot run well in the midst of it all unless now and then we run away from it all.

It is good to be home again—and in October!

2 WHITTLING

I'M out on the front porch at home, looking across this gorgeous autumn landscape to the distant skyline, where at night the lights of five little towns run along like footlights of a stage. On the west the Blue Ridge Mountains are almost lost in this Indian summer haze. Last week I bought for myself this old home by the side of the road, and I dream big dreams of a quiet retreat on top of this hill, far from the madding crowd's ignoble strife.

I've been whittling while I loaf, making tiny baskets from the plentiful acorns. No value, of course, just a pastime; and yet more valuable than many things I've done. I do not smoke. I know that Spurgeon did, but I have never been able to see how I could make a cuspidor of my mouth and a chimney of my nose to the glory of God. There are better ways of doing nothing, clean and wholesome. One of them is whittling.

Whittling is a lost art in this efficient age. Everybody is too busy going nowhere in a hurry. But I doubt not that in the good old days many an important problem was solved with a knife and a stick of wood. Abe Lincoln must have pared down many a knotty issue in this homely fashion. But, of course, he didn't have to hurry around to radio broadcasts, *et cetera ad infinitum.*

Said Newton D. Baker: "The effect of modem inventions has been to immeasurably increase the difficulty of deliberation and contemplation about large and important issues. I doubt whether there could have been a Constitution of the United States of America if the deliberations of the Constitutional Convention had been currently reported by radio, telegraph and timely newspapers over the whole extent of the thirteen colonies."

Quite so! I am convinced that those old worthies must have whittled out more than one decision. When I was preaching in Park Street Church in Boston, I meandered one day in that old, old graveyard where lie the bodies of Paul Revere and other notables of that heroic age. It required little imagination to picture those celebrities carving out patterns from wood while they pondered weightier concerns!

One would think that in a day of such scientific skill and wonders of invention there would be a proportionate increase in human character. But, alas, man has become the Punch and Judy of his own show. And he has forgotten how to whittle. He cannot endure being alone, for then he is in such poor company. If he endeavors to relax, he must be in a honky-tonk or watching other people play from a stadium seat. He cannot be still and know God.

It shows up in things spiritual. Samuel Rutherford, Robert Murray McCheyne, John Bunyan, would be brushed aside today by church workers headed for another committee meeting. Whether or not they whittled, I cannot say, but they took time out and lost no time in so doing. They would win no prizes today in your modem church-efficiency program, but they knew God.

And, then, there are others today who are too busy doing things of importance. Satan is clever. If he cannot put God's servant to sleep, he works him into a St. Vitus dance and then brings him down in a crash to the dishonor of the cause. These, too, should learn to whittle now and then.

Mix your work and worship with a little whittling. It pays.

3 COUNTRY PREACHING

YESTERDAY I preached at Corinth, the old home church here in the hills. There is now a new stone building, and a modern highway goes by; but still there gather around that hallowed spot memories of other years when life was plainer. In reverie I go up the old dirt road again in father's buggy or the old surrey. Again I draw near the little wooden church in the grove in "big-meetin' time," when the evening service starts at "early candlelight."

I hear the stamping of horses tethered all over the grove. Hound dogs are in abundance. The farmer folk have gathered, the men in overalls, the women quite often in gingham and calico. There are crying babies galore, for they were still in style back before lap poodles were substituted for lawful progeny.

Presently some one raises the tune within the church and singing begins to the accompaniment of the wheezy old organ. They could not have passed muster at a radio audition, but they knew how to make a joyful noise unto the Lord. "Amazing Grace," "Brethren, We Have Met to Worship," and other old classics peal forth—and, of course, "There Is a Fountain Filled with Blood," for the blood songs had not yet been dropped from hymnals because modem skeptics laugh at a blood- bought redemption.

There followed an "experience-meeting," when the saints told how it was grace that made their hearts to fear and grace their fears relieved, and then wait on to relate how precious did that grace appear the hour they first believed. There were tears and "amens" for, to use Finney's phrase, Mr. Wet-Eyes and Mr. Amen were still in the congregation.

Came next the sermon, and that was back in the days of beefsteak preaching, not your modem handing out of moral nicknacks and spiritual sandwiches. Knowing the terror of the Lord, those old worthies persuaded men, the love of Christ constraining them. They knew both the goodness and severity of the Lord, and never hesitated to preach from such texts as, ^u He that being often reproved hardeneth his neck shall suddenly be destroyed and that without remedy."

They sang, "I am coming to the cross, I am poor and weak and blind," and the sinners filled the mourner's bench, confessing their sins. In those days they still believed they had sins to confess; and when they got into trouble, they had not learned to hire an alienist to blame their misdeeds on their grandfathers and hang their guilt on their family tree.

It was no uncommon thing to see the "mourners" rise from their knees, shouting in joy of sins forgiven and burdens lifted. Oh, I see you smile in condescending tolerance and ascribe such things to an age of ignorance, and pass it up with a psychological explanation. Well, we are in no position today to throw stones from our house of glass. Any generation that has landed in as big a muddle as we are in today had better save its dunce cap for itself. For further information, read your morning newspaper!

I'm not the only pilgrim who is weary in all this modern much ado about nothing. There is plenty of homesickness today, not just for "the good old times," for we have sense enough to know we can't turn backward Time in its flight. There is a longing for something we lost back there that we had better find again. If we were convicted enough, conscious of sin enough, humble enough, desperate enough, we might find it again. We have hewn out broken cisterns that can hold no water. But still He stands as in days of old to say, "If any man thirst, let him come unto me and drink."

4 A FRIEND OF GOD

I HAVE been reading from the *Journal of David Brainerd,* that American saint, preacher to the Indians, prevailer in prayer. I am quite sure that the average modem efficient American would promptly dismiss David Brainerd from his mind if ever he heard of him (which he hasn't, being far better posted on movie actors and football stars); such a seeker after God among us today would be classed an interesting psychological specimen, an introspective neurotic headed for a psychopathic ward.

Well, here is a sample from the life of this friend of God, and whether or not this is familiar language to us as we read it will determine what world we move in:

"Prayed privately with a dear Christian friend or two; and I think I scarce ever launched so far into the eternal world as then. I got so far out on the broad ocean that my soul with joy triumphed over all the evils on the shores of mortality. I think that time and all its gay amusements and cruel disappointments never appeared so inconsiderable to me before."

Is that an unknown tongue to you, or have you been there too? For all our vaunted progress, what have we in this modern masquerade that will match that? We have gained the world and lost our souls. A race of prodigals in the far country fain would feed itself with the husks that swine do eat and yet thinks itself rich and needing nothing. But all the wealth of today is only trinkets and toys, shavings and sawdust, beside what this dying man found alone in the wilderness with God. And for all our schools and churches, our bustling efficiency and boasted prestige, the preacher who really thirsts after God goes back to light his taper at such a flame as Brainerd's, which burned itself out in thirty years.

Brainerd knew God, and to know God through Christ is the supreme privilege of every soul. Anyone can know God and walk with Him day by day. It is not the peculiar right of ascetics and cloistered saints who have nothing else to do. Business man and housewife, rich and poor, whether on the boulevard or in the backwoods—any man may know God.

But not many do. Alas, not many in our churches. A certain amount of church work on Sunday, a duplex envelope on the plate every Lord's Day, that is not knowing God. Alas, there are preachers who know not God. The signpost points to the city but never goes there. One may point toward heaven and never enter its gates. Bunyan perceived that there was a way to hell from the gate of heaven. Saddest of all will it be to hear our Lord say to men who have prophesied and cast out devils, "Depart ... I NEVER KNEW YOU." There is a strait gate and a narrow way that leads to life and FEW there be that find it.

And so many who have had a work of grace done in their souls know God so poorly. For it takes time to be holy, and it takes work, and it takes tears and sweat and travail and study and self-denial and diligent application, and all these things are now out of date. Men come to a light profession with untroubled hearts, for grace has never taught their hearts to fear; and they pursue their way without joy, for grace has not their fears relieved. To know and love and serve God is not their chief concern; nay, is it a concern at all? Yet it should be our main business, and our earthly trade or profession merely a means of living while we learn to know Him and make Him known. How Satan has snared us from this chief pursuit, and if he can do no worse with us he engages us with religious activities to keep us from walking with God.

Enoch walked with God. "That I may know him" was Paul's chief concern. It was David Brainerd's. Set yourself diligently to make it yours.

5 PICKANINNY

I WAS strolling out to church late one Sunday afternoon. Down the road before me, ambling carelessly along, a Negro man carried fondly in his arms a baby, its chocolate face turned over his shoulder toward me, its wide eyes staring in innocent wonder at everything in sight.

I was in a mellow mood and "mammy's little coal-black rose" stirred tender reflections. After all, mused the strolling parson, are not we both, pickaninny and preacher, only wondering children given a few short years to spend in this strange world together? From one great mystery we came to live awhile on a puzzling earth and then move on to the mightiest wonder of all. How little he knows of life's tangles; yet, do I know much more?

He is on his way to some obscure little shanty. How little he has and yet how much is his! About all that really matters is his as well as mine. For him the sky is blue, the sun is warm, the grass is green; for him the wood thrush sings from the cypresses at sundown. For him the sunbeams dance as freely as for pampered sons of wealth, the violet blooms as readily by his cabin door. The breezes kiss his cheeks impartially; the mocking bird sings his choicest bars as gaily for this dusky listener as for kings and princes. For him the seasons work their magic wonders. The whole wide universe was made and the mighty process of the ages rolls on as surely for him as for me.

And then I think that life is his—life, eternal mystery of the ages that no scientist can trap, no philosopher explain; strange spark from somewhere else; no mortal wit can make it, no wealth can buy it, nor can all the wise men bring it back when it is gone. Yet that priceless treasure belongs to the pickaninny as truly as to me.

And health is his. Dyspeptics and diseased millionaires with burned-out stomachs would gladly be poor again for this baby's appetite, which, doubtless, knows no bounds. He might have millions if he chose to sell and could!

Yes, even more: Is not God as near to him as to any saint in cloistered cathedral? Does not the Father bend over him in solicitude strong and tender? Is he any less precious because carved in ebony instead of ivory? It is no farther from his shanty to heaven than from my church. God is his now in innocency, for he is God's; and when he is grown, all that God offers is for him as well as for me.

It was for him that Jesus came and lived and died; for him Bethlehem and Calvary and the open grave. He has a part in that matchless provision. He may be cheated out of much, but no man can take that from him if he cheat not himself. And if he lay hold upon it, all things are his. He may never own a foot of earth, but if he belong to the blessed meek he will inherit it all.

Thus mused the preacher about the pickaninny— and finally came to earth with a practical conclusion. For was not the little tot, though he wondered at all he saw, simply trusting in his father's arms? His wide-eyed amazement at the sights he passed did not in the least affect his utter trust. Ah, that I, while I ponder over this and that, beset with problems I cannot fathom, every day brought up against enigmas I cannot understand—that I may never let the mystery around me hinder my repose in the Everlasting Arms I Did He not say we must become as little children? So would I move along life's winding lane, as restful as a child in parental arms, and, in spite of strange things along the way, serenely confident that I am going Home.

6 IF YOU ARE NERVOUS

THERE are two kinds of people, nervous ad those who laugh at nervous. And never the twain shall meet decent understanding, for nervous people can't understand how everybody else can be so cheerful, and those who aren't nervous can't see why anybody should feel so queer. The only person who can really understand the strange pranks of jaded nerves is he who has been along that road himself and, being delivered, can comfort others with the comfort wherewith he himself has been comforted of God. Ye fellow pilgrims, who know the language of insomnia and the blues, suffer a word from a qualified companion in tribulation.

If you have been beset with all those symptoms that can be felt but not described; if you have counted more sheep than America owes dollars; if you have known that nameless fear that settles like a fog and you divide your time between fearing you won't die and fearing you will, don't leave Nathanael's fig tree for Elijah's juniper I However, there is this much comfort to be drawn from the juniper: if even rugged Elijah came down with a nervous reaction after his big day at Carmel, we lesser fry need not be surprised if ofttimes the journey is too great for us. No man can stay at high pitch all the time: of course, Elijah should not have run from Jezebel, but even that is better than running toward her, as they did in Thyatira! And, mind you, the Lord did not give Elijah a lecture: He fed him and put him to sleep, then He led him to the experience of the still, small voice. What tunes the devil can play on tense, overpitched nerves, until we fancy ourselves the lone survivors of all the good men of earth I In such a time be not harsh with yourself. If God was not harsh with Elijah, we might follow His example with ourselves. Instead of further straining with tortuous exercises of mind or soul, doubtless we should take food and rest. And then, past fire and whirlwind and earthquake, to hear the still, small voice. Resting for God is as important as working for God. We often do more by doing less. "Come ye apart," said the Lord—and if we don't come apart, we will come apart! God is not interested in our quantity production but in quality, and frazzled workers can easily spoil their message by their manner.

The Elijah of the New Testament, John the Baptist, fared much like his predecessor of old. In jail, he plunged into doubt and depression and sent a delegation to the Lord questioning the very thing he had preached with all the fearlessness of a lion. Once again, observe that our Lord did not lecture John the Baptist nor send him a sweet little treatise on "How to Be Happy in Jail." Jesus made His finest remarks about John right when John had made his poorest remarks about Jesus! Truly, He knoweth our frame and remembereth that we are dust.

The choicest of saints have trodden the way of the two Elijahs. Read John Bunyan and check up on Cowper. Dear James McConkey could comfort others because he had a lifelong warfare against gloom. Hear Spurgeon: "Trapp says, 'David chideth David out of the dumps.' Why this depression, this chicken-hearted melancholy?" Even in their last hours A. J. Gordon and A. B. Simpson wrestled against despair. Dr. Torrey had his two years of insomnia.

But more of this later. This chapter is just to get acquainted. Of course, if you aren't bothered with these troubles you won't be interested. But if you're in this dungeon you'd read through a dictionary to find your way out. There is a way. And you'll come out with a feeling for fellow prisoners that no other school could ever teach you. And that is one reason why we are allowed to get in!

7 THIS WAY OUT

IF you are in the dumps, perhaps the trouble is physical. Maybe it is your stomach and not your soul that needs fixing. Don't further irritate your spirit by morbid prodding if your digestion and not your devotion is at fault. Remember the old Negro mammy who was in an automobile wreck. Of course, where there's a wreck there's a lawyer, and he said, "Auntie, you ought to collect some damages from this," "Damages!" she retorted. "Man, I'se done collected enough damages, what Ah needs is repairs!"

So have a thorough check-up and do as you are told. But maybe the trouble is mental. In that case you'll need some stiff straightening out of your thought habits and it won't be done overnight. But we press on to the spiritual, for if you are set right there, the mental and physical can be made to fall inline.

Make sure, first of all, of your salvation. That is simple enough; it is we who have made it complicated. A lady asked me, "Do you have to have an experience to be saved?" "I answered, "Yes, but what do you *mean by an* experience? On what are you depending now for your salvation?" "I *am* depending on *Christ,*" she answered, "on *the* ground of His finished work on Calvary." "Then," I answered, "is not that an experience?" I think she had the idea that she must go through a certain emotional upset such as she had seen in some one else in order to be saved. Now, the emotions have their place and a real experience of God's grace will affect intelligence, will and emotions, all three. *Hut* leave the effect with the Lord, and remember that if you ever came *to* Christ as best you knew bow, realizing yourself to be helplessly and hopelessly lost without Him and simply trusting Him to save and keep you, He has promised that He will not cast you out. Let His Word be enough, for

"What more can He say than to you He hath said,

To you who for refuge to Jesus have fled?"

Don't worry over whether you have repented enough or believed enough or wept enough or prayed enough. Nothing you could ever do would be enough. Jesus is enough, and if you have turned yourself over to Him, lock, stock and barrel, remember He will keep all you commit. I might believe in a bank and walk up and down the street, saying," I believe In the bank, I believe in the bank," but the bank will not keep my money unless

I deposit it. So saving faith must be faith that commits, but if you have committed as best you knew and if you meant business, don't lose any sleep for fear heaven will go bankrupt and God go insolvent. Paul didn't say, "I know bow I fed," but "I know whom I have believed and I am persuaded that he is able to keep that which I have committed unto him against that day." You see, it was faith that committed.

"Three ran were walking on a wall;

Feeling, Faith and Fact;

Feeling got an awful fall

And Faith was taken back;

Faith was so close to Feeling,

He fell too;

But Fact remained and pulled Faith up,

And that brought Feeling too!"

Whoever wrote that knew the Way Out!

His blood makes safe, His Word makes sure. And "the soul that on Jesus hath leaned for repose, He will not, He will not desert to its foes." The Negro brother who had just taken his first airplane ride said, "It was all right, but I never did put down all my weight while I was up there."

Put down all your weight, the Foundation stand- eth sure!

This Way Out is simply HIS WAY OUT!

8 WHAT TO DO

IF you have full assurance of salvation, and yet you are in a dungeon, make sure that all you are and have is fully yielded to God. Back of much of our moods and misery there is a point of rebellion against God. "He that covereth his sins shall not prosper; but whoso confesseth and forsaketh them shall have mercy" (Prov. 28:13). Mind you, they must not only be confessed but forsaken. No matter how much is involved, there must be a removal of the cause, for there cannot be soul health if the festering sore of wilful sin keeps poisoning the life. But the minute you have confessed the sin and put it away, believe that He has forgiven according to His promise (1 John 1:8), and do not wallow in regret and remorse.

Perhaps it is some doubtful matter. You cannot make up your mind whether it is right or wrong. In that case, remember another word: "He that doubteth is condemned if he eat, because he eateth not of faith: for whatsoever is not of faith is sin" (Rom. 14: 23). If there is a question mark after it, give God the benefit of the doubt. You will never lose by giving God the long end of any proposition.

If you have honestly done all this and still you are under the juniper, do not worry for fear there is something God is holding against you that you do not know about. If you honestly will to do God's will, you shall know not only of the doctrine but anything else you need to know if you let the Spirit speak to you through the Word and prayer and any other avenue He may choose. But remember that whatever He says will be in line with the Word. There are other spirits, but they contradict the Word.

If you humbly and honestly wait on the Lord and no trouble is revealed, then it is the devil, the accuser of the saints, who is trying to make you miserable. He will discourage and depress and confuse you if he can for he is out to steal the joy of your salvation and keep you off the firing line occupied with yourself, ever learning and never able to come to the knowledge of the truth, always taking your own pulse and temperature. If God has revealed no point of rebellion, you must conclude that there is none, and then turn on the devil with the shield of faith and sword of the Word and order him off the premises. Don't let the mosquito accusations of the adversary cheat you out of enjoying the Lord.

And do not forget that if you are to grow strong in the Lord, you must obey the laws of growth. Sometimes it is not sins of commission but of omission. To grow, you must eat, rest, and exercise, feed on the Word, rest in the Lord, exercise unto godliness. There are too many shade-tree saints and rocking-chair Christians. If we fed our bodies as we feed our souls and exercised our limbs as we exercise our spirits, we would have wound up in a sanitarium long ago. There is too much silly imagining that the Christian life is a queer, ethereal, unreal sort of dream. It is a wholesome, practical matter, and God has not given us the spirit of fear but of power and of love and of a sound mind, and "sound mind" here means discipline, sound judgment.

You say, "I've heard all that before." Exactly. That's just it. We know it in our heads, but we are too careless or lazy to work it out; we want something lovely to sweep over our feelings, answer all our questions, fight all our battles. But we are soldiers and salvation is a helmet, not a nightcap. I know you've heard it before. What are you doing about it?

"If ye know these things, happy are ye if ye do them."

9 "LET HIM ASK IN FAITH"

FOR a long, long time I misused that precious promise: "If any of you lack wisdom, let him ask of God, that giveth to all men liberally, and upbraideth not; and it shall be given him" (James 1:5).

I certainly needed wisdom. And here was a plain promise from a liberal God that wisdom would be given. So I prayed. But when I rose, things looked just about the same. The room had not changed. The world appeared about as it was when I closed my eyes. And inside I felt as usual. I certainly felt no wiser. If only the Lord would send a special delivery letter and tell me just what to do! So I wandered along, uncertainly, hoping with Mr. Micawber that "something would turn up."

And then one day I saw my own picture—right in the Bible. For the Lord had put it right after the very verse about praying for wisdom. "But let him ask in faith, nothing wavering. For he that wavereth is like a wave of the sea driven with the wind and tossed. For let not that man think that he shall receive anything of the Lord. A double minded man is unstable in all his ways." Weymouth's translation only made the picture stand out clearer: "A person of that sort must not expect to receive anything from the Lord, being a man of two minds, undecided in every step he takes!"

And why was I such a wobbler? Because I had not asked in faith. Right here is the fundamental weakness in this problem of guidance. Nothing seems to baffle believers more than how to know the will of God. The question is fired at us from meeting to meeting.

And yet the whole matter boils down to this: If you need wisdom on any matter, look first into the Word. Sometimes it covers the matter explicitly. For instance, one would know from the Bible that a Christian should not marry an unbeliever. At other times, the general principle is laid down that covers specific cases. For instance, anything that offends a weaker brother is outlawed.

If the Word allows liberty to decide either way, as it often does in many matters where right and wrong are not involved, make sure that you are willing to do either way the Lord directs. Two-thirds of the battle is right there. If you are ready to take either fork of the road, most of the trouble is over. Then circumstances and sanctified judgment and advice of more experienced Christians may be consulted.

In the light of all this, having asked God for wisdom with a willing heart, yon have a right to rise from your knees believing that God will assist you in the decision you make. Make the decision that you honestly feel to be best and trust God to check or correct it if you should be wrong. God will not let you down. It is even better to make some mistakes than to be "a man of two minds undecided in every step he takes." In making a decision, you give God a chance at least to correct it. Indecision gives God no chance at all. "Let not that man think that he shall receive anything of the Lord."

God knows when you mean business. If your first desire is to please Him, He knows it and He will not let you go far wrong. It is better to make some blunders in faith than the supreme blunder of unbelief. To walk in faith is the only real success; to walk in doubt the only real failure.

10 "I BELIEVE GOD"

I BELIEVE God, that it shall be even as it was told me." So said Paul in the storm at sea. To all appearances the situation was hopeless: "All hope that we should be saved was then taken away." But Paul had word from heaven and so hoped against hope.

This whole matter of Christian living is simply one issue: believing God. And that boils down to believing the Bible. Even John 3: 16 depends on 2 Timothy 3: 16, for if all Scripture is not God-breathed, then I may doubt any of it.

God has expressed Himself on sin. I believe God. I believe Him for salvation. I believe Him for assurance. I believe Him for sanctification. I believe Him for the filling of the Spirit. For health, food, clothes, money, my future, I believe God. "Abraham believed God and it was counted to him for righteousness." And so must I. "For we walk by faith, not by sight."

It is not merely believing there is a God. The devils believe and tremble, and we don't even tremble It is not merely believing in God, that He is all He says. That is better, but it is not saving faith.

We must believe God enough to "take Him up on it," to let our lives be a sermon on the text, " Let God be true but every man a liar." It is a matter of believing, regardless of anything inside or outside, feel like it or not. I think of the old-time Methodist preacher who went to camp meeting. He had a great time, shouted his tongue out and his collar down. Next day one of his flock remarked, "You don't feel as good today as you did yesterday." "No," the old saint replied, "but I believe today just like I did yesterday I" He believed God.

Believing God means believing Christ, for no man comes to the Father but by the Son. "Ye believe God, believe also in me." And believing Christ is to live positively. There is health and victory in being a human exclamation point; but a human question mark breeds sin and sickness and sorrow. Negative, uncertain, doubtful living poisons body, mind, and spirit; fills insane asylums, penitentiaries, graves, hell itself. "Love thinketh no evil," and to believe God is to believe the best always about everyone and everything until we must believe the worst. But negative poor souls always fore-fancy the worst and then grudgingly acknowledge the best. Better believe in some one and be disappointed than never to believe at all.

No man can be saved until he believes God about salvation and acts accordingly. And no Christian can ever know a life of joy and power and victory until he snaps out of the vicious circle of half-believing and half-doubting and moves from negation or interrogation to affirmation. "To me to live is Christ," and when Christ lives within He believes God!

"He hath said ... so that we may boldly say." He hath not said so that we may guess about it, hope so, but that we may hilariously and dangerously and boldly say "I believe God, that it shall be even as it was told me."

Throw your doubts to the winds, stand on your feelings, laugh at your circumstances, though you sometimes feel like a fool doing it. The devil will scare you out of it if he can, but although, as with Paul, the storm may rage and all hope seem out of the question, let the world know that you have had word from higher quarters, and shout in the teeth of the gale, "I believe God." Oh, there may be hardship ahead: "Howbeit, we must be cast upon a certain island" was Paul's next word. But, mind you, although the ship was wrecked, Paul was not wrecked nor anything God had promised him. It shall be as He has told us.

11 PARTING

I HAVE just returned from the funeral of my mother. We carried her up to the little country church, where the kindly farmfolk neighbors paid their last respects. They sang "How Firm a Foundation," and how precious it was, old-fashioned people singing an old-fashioned song at the funeral of an old-fashioned mother.

They sang her favorite, "Meet Me There," and I am so glad that in such an hour, however the skeptics may laugh, faith knows there is a land that is fairer than day, for it is by faith that we see it afar. And I am glad that in such a time my heart can say:

"Death can hide but not divide;

Thou art but on Christ's other side.

Thou art with Christ and Christ with me;

In Christ united still are we."

And now I'm back at the old home on the hill and out in the gathering twilight looking across the hills to where the sun went down. Somehow, it is easy this evening almost to dose the eyes and fancy one sees beyond the sunset the inviting portals of another world. This evening it is easy—and what a heart relief—to sing:

"O think of the home over there,

By the side of the river of light,

Where the saints, all immortal and fair,

Are robed in their garments of white."

I've been rummaging in the old dresser drawer where she kept the letters I wrote and treasured little remembrances like the birthday cards I sent her. They tell me that as the day of her passing drew nearer, she read her Bible more, and often they found her by the radio listening to some Gospel message with the countenance of those who are nearer to the next world than to this.

Hers was a Scotch-Irish inheritance, with a simple faith and a plain philosophy that have grown exceedingly scarce in this lollipop age. I have heard of an old lady who had gotten such a blessing from the verse, "I will never leave thee nor forsake thee" (Heb. 13: 5). When a certain Greek scholar sought to add to her enjoyment by telling her that she might freely translate it, "I'll never, no never, no never, forsake thee," she replied, "Well, the Lord may have to say it three times before you scholars can get it, but once is enough for me!" My mothers faith was something like that.

God's Word speaks of "joy and peace in believing" (Rom. 15: 13), and further reminds us, "If ye will not believe, surely ye shall not be established" (Isa. 7: 9). Satisfaction, serenity, stability, all these come by faith, faith in Christ the Fact, and these were the marks of our believing mothers.

Hers was a faith that brought courage. Her last word to me while I was away in the North preaching was dictated to my brother as he wrote: "Tell him to keep up the good fight, for God is with him, and 'if God be for us, who can be against us?'"

In that spirit we carry on.

12 A STROLLER IN SNOW

I HAVE been outdoors all morning, tramping through the fresh snow, thrilled with the spotless beauty of a white world and half humming to myself those exquisite lines of Lowell:

> "The snow had begun in the gloaming
>
> And busily all the night
>
> Had been heaping field and highway
>
> With a silence deep and white.
>
> Every pine and fir and hemlock
>
> Wore ermine too dear for an earl;
>
> And the poorest twig on the elm tree
>
> Was ridged inch-deep in pearl."

He who has never trudged through pine woods after a snowfall, who has not felt his face tingle in the crisp breeze nor known the zest and tang of this crowning glory of winter, has not really lived. I drank, without bending, from clusters of snow in the tops of the pine shrubs—no filter, no machine, just the frozen fountains the Lord made without one human "improvement."

I went to a favorite spot that might well be called the Pine Temple: spotless aisles, softer than any plush; with pines as sturdy columns, their tops snow-woven into designs only heaven can create; and, above all, the azure sky dome. To some it might be only a patch of woods, but today it is a Snow Sanctuary, a cathedral fit for angels.

Out there I dropped the luggage of life and merged for awhile back into the elemental world from whence I came. It is good for a man to escape to these silences once in a while and remember what he is and whence he came. It is not good to stay always amidst the traffic of earth's market place, lest in the fever of buying and selling he endanger his soul.

So I grew calm and rested and my brow unwrinkled and my perspective untangled, and my cares, like the Arabs, stole away. Above me chattered the chickadees, the optimists of the winter woods; near by the jaunty titmouse bravely whistled and the tiny kinglets, ruggedest little mites that ever wore feathers, worked busily, while the nuthatches explored tree trunks head-downward, and peaceful snowbirds (whoever started calling them juncos?) sedately enjoyed the snow world they love.

Back home at last, in a snug chair before a warm fire, I thought of Whittier's *Snow Bound*. He little dreamed that his simple picture of a New England home in the setting of a winter landscape would meet instant success, bringing fame and fortune in its train. He had struck a chord that reverberates wherever one muses before an open fire, shut in by a snow world outside.

So I came to bedtime with another snow thought resting like a benediction, the sweetest of them all: David's prayer, "Wash me and I shall be whiter than snow," and, in reply, God's assurance in Isaiah, "Though your sins be as scarlet, they shall be as white as snow." Vain are all those Pilates who would wash away their guilt in waters of this earth. Vain are all Naamans who would trust in Abana and Pharpar. "Though thou wash thee with nitre and take thee much soap, yet thine iniquity is marked before me, saith the Lord God." But though infidelity may erase it from our hymn books, we still can sing:

> "What can wash away my sin?

Nothing but the blood of Jesus."

13 WAKE UP!

DID you ever read a chapter in your morning devotions and then suddenly realize afterward that you couldn't remember one single verse of it? Did you ever try to pray and instantly all the things you had meant to do and had forgotten suddenly popped into your mind? (A very good way to refresh your memory on other matters is to try praying.) Did you ever go to church and find it almost impossible to concentrate on the sermon and you came home wondering whether you were sick or backsliding?

Not necessarily either. We are living in the last days and perilous times, and we are up against an atmosphere that no Christians of earlier ages ever encountered. Add to that the fact that we are a shallow and superficial generation any way you take it and you can begin to put two and two together.

Somebody has written a timely word about the matter that runs like this: In the last days "all kinds of strange feelings and new and peculiar trials will come to us. A surprising lack of desire and energy God ward, a spiritual deadness, a mental heaviness, lethargy of soul, an alarming desire for forbidden things and a peculiar delight and fascination in any of the world's pleasures we dare taste. It will be difficult to preach the Word in liberty and power; it will be difficult to give attention to the Word when it is preached; it will be very difficult to get down to real earnest and continued prayer."

Paul certainly was not indulging in mere figures of speech when he wrote that we wrestle not against flesh and blood but against spiritual powers in the heavenlies. It never was harder to apply oneself to eternal concerns and stir up the gift of God than today. The very atmosphere is dull and drowsy. The devil makes our eyelids heavy, fills our minds with cobwebs, and while the spirit may be willing the flesh is weak. We must take ourselves by the back of the neck and shake ourselves from this coma and lethargy, for we have been cocained and chloroformed by the spirit of this ungodly age.

> "In vain we tune our formal songs;
>
> In vain we strive to rise;
>
> Hosannas languish on our tongues
>
> And our devotion dies."

We had better dispense with some of our frothy church jingles and sing:

> "My soul, be on thy guard;
>
> Ten thousand foes arise;
>
> The hosts of sin are pressing hard
>
> To draw thee from the skies."

Sometime ago, in using this dear old hymn, I said « A thousand foes arise," and then noticed that I had missed it by nine thousand! But George Heath did not put the number too high.

You need not be surprised, my believing brother, if you find yourself ofttimes beset with a strange stupor. It is at least encouraging that the devil gives you his attention. Some are already so completely under his sway that he leaves them alone and they will see no point in this little discourse, if they have not already dropped it to pick up their love-story magazine.

But of course you are not to drowse off into sleep on this account. Gird on your armor and fight the good fight of faith as you never fought it before! Watch that you may pray and pray that you may watch! "Awake my soul, stretch every nerve and press with vigor on." Let that be your theme song! "Awake to righteousness and sin not!" "It is high time to awake out of sleep, for now is our salvation nearer than when we believed!"

14 THREE D'S

IN the New Testament family album three men whose names begin with the same letter stand out as typical of three kinds of Christians today. The Scripture account of them all is very brief, but a little window lets in much light and from the meagre record we immediately recognize that their kind has not yet disappeared from the earth.

There was Demas, who forsook Paul, having loved this present world (2 Tim. 4: 10). Doubtless he had started out in dead earnest, maybe with plenty of fire, but the pull of the old life and the charm of the world were too much for him. Think not, however, of Demas merely as the sort lured away today by dances and movies. Certainly all that belongs to this present world, but we are in danger of restricting "worldliness" to a few pet evils, forgetting that what is in mind here is the age in which Demas lived. The spirit of the times got him, and he got into the tempo of it, was carried away with the surge of it. One may not be a bridge fiend and yet may be worldly; he need not drink cocktails to be in the same boat with Demas. Active church workers, free from the grosser sins and unaffiliated with the fun and frolic of low living may, nevertheless, still be worldlings. The Christian's citizenship is in heaven and whatever does not savor of that is of the world. Any interest that gets ahead of the will of God, be it business or pleasure or ambition; any concern that interferes with Paul's "this one thing I do" is of Demas and of the devil.

Then, there was Diotrephes, who loved the preeminence (3John 9). He lived in the days of the primitive church, before the false distinction between clergy and laity had become established. But he was a "dog-in-the-manger" sort, who lorded it over the brethren, opposed dear, saintly old John, and refused the visiting ministers, assuming an authority not taught in the Word. His sort is still with us in the minister who bosses instead of shepherds his flock; in ecclesiastical overlords who reject all visiting brethren who do not measure up to their private yardstick; in any and all who want to rule instead of serve. We are in no danger of running short today in the supply of Diotrephes. It is a day of apostasy and we could identify it by this mark if by no other. The third epistle of John is a little, one-page guidebook for the believer in such a time, and loving the pre-eminence is a prevailing sin of the age.

And forget not that loving the pre-eminence is as bad as loving this present world, indeed, it amounts to the same thing. Many a Pharisee who would not think of living like Demas ends up in as bad company with Diotrephes. Many churches today have an equal representation in the two: on the one hand, an army of worldlings at home down in Egypt [11] preferring a taste of garlic to a foretaste of glory"; on the other, a band of dissenters and dividers rending the assembly over Paul and Apollos and Cephas. Poor Demas usually is fired at aplenty by the evangelists, and he deserves it; but do not use up all your ammunition, my brother, on cards and dancing; save a generous portion for "strife, envyings and divisions," the Bible-certified marks of carnality!

How refreshing it is to move from these two troublesome souls to Demetrius, who loved the truth (3 John 12). Whether or not he was the Ephesian silversmith, now converted, he had good report of all and of the truth and of John; and his sort is altogether too rare today. He was no celebrity, but we could profitably exchange some of our striking personalities for more of his kind. What would the church do today without his quiet, faithful, steadying testimony? God help us in such a time to choose the

Demetrius way of good report and not the Diotrephes way of loud report!

15 "A WAY OUT OF NO WAY"

WHEN I was a pastor in quaint, historic old Charleston, I numbered among my friends one Adam Brown. He was an aged Negro preacher who conducted a little orphanage on Wadmalaw Island. He was such a typical low-country Negro that he got his picture into the *National Geographic Magazine* in a write-up of Charleston.

It was his custom to visit me about once a week. I could distinguish his footfall along the hotel hallway from that of any other caller. When I opened the door, there he stood in garments as original as his own wit and philosophy. A sort of interdenominational outfit consisting of a straw hat in winter, an Episcopalian collar, and a Methodist coat, was Adam Brown's.

Before we engaged in any conversation, his first word always was, "Let us pray." He usually prefaced his prayer with a verse or two from some old, old hymn he had stored in his mind and heart until it was part of himself. And how he could half recite, half sing it, with a real beauty no school of expression could ever give.

Then he would launch into his prayer, and here he was on no strange territory. It was evident that he had been often out of this world and up in heaven. And that he understood much of the nature of Divine dealings was evident in a prayer for me one morning. I was starting out on a preaching trip. Adam Brown prayed: "Lord, bless our brother; make a way for him; MAKE A WAY OUT OF NO WAY!"

Now, that is just what God does. He who hung the earth upon nothing, He who chooses things that are not as His instruments, delights in making a way where there is none. In making old Abraham the father of a great nation, in opening the waters of the Red Sea, in crumbling Jericho's walls at the sound of a shout, in manifold deliverances of His saints throughout the Book and down to this good day, He makes a way out of no way! One thinks of the little girl describing her first train ride: "We came to a lake and I was 'most scared to death. We ran right into it, but it was all right. Somebody had gone ahead and built a bridge over it!" How often have we seemed to plunge into this chasm and that abyss—but Some One had gone ahead and built a bridge!

Adam Brown's understanding of providential grace is sadly needed by many whose wealth or station or learning would not suffer them to condescend to one of such low estate. But God has a name for keeping His secrets from the wise and prudent and revealing them to babes. When I want an illustration of real faith I go to a Christian "darky," for he believes, while the rest of us study faith and write books about it. It is true, as David Grayson said, that a colored man can do more with less and less with much than anyone else in the world. But if godliness with contentment is great gain, your believing Aunt Mandy is a spiritual millionaire. And having learned humility, the Negro is spared much humiliation.

> "He that is down need fear no fall;
>
> He that is low, no pride;
>
> He that is humble ever shall
>
> Have God to be his guide."

These are they who travel the "way out of no way." For they walk by faith, not by sight.

16 "NOT SO, LORD"

LOT said it (Gen. 19: 18). The angels of the Lord had bidden him flee to a mountain to escape Sodom. Instead, he asked to be allowed to escape to the little town of Zoar. It was only a little place, he reasoned. God graciously granted his request, but later he had to flee to the mountain after all, and the man who did not have room enough in the whole country when he was with Abraham ended in what Matthew Henry called a "hole in the hill."

This strange, puzzling man, righteous at heart, was never truly separated from the world unto God. Although he had the root of the matter in him, he pitched toward Sodom, and although he got rich there and sat in the city council, he paid for his folly in the morals of his daughters and seemed as one that mocked unto his sons-in-law. He never was in the perfect will of God and his life was keyed to that note of rebellion: "Not so, my Lord."

The number of those who walk in his ways today is legion. They choose their own refuge instead of God's best; they start out to profit themselves instead of to please Him; they live in the Sodom of this age, doomed to judgment; and when it comes, they cannot give it up altogether but still hold out for Zoar. We call them "worldly Christians" in our churches, but at heart they are rebels, for the friend of this world is labeled in the Book "the enemy of God." The main trouble is not that they dance and play cards and are in the theatre on prayer-meeting night. The deeper trouble is inward rebellion against the will of God: "Not so, my Lord."

But our phrase occurs again, this time in the New Testament. Peter sees the vision of the vessel filled with beasts, fowls, and creeping things. He is bidden, "Rise, Peter, kill and eat." Peter objected: "Not so, Lord; for I have never eaten anything that is common or unclean." The voice replies: "What God hath cleansed, that call not thou common."

Lot was not separated enough. Peter was too separated. He had yet to learn that "every creature of God is good and nothing to be refused if it be received with thanksgiving, for it is sanctified by the word of God and prayer." He was a Jew and his ceremonial convictions had to be converted to grace by a special revelation. You will remember that his attitude showed up at Antioch.

Peter was an honest Jew and there was some reason for his argument. But today there are those who have fallen for the "Touch not, Taste not, Handle not" heresy and in their reaction against worldliness have gone too far in separation. They move about in an air of superior sanctity, in Pharisaic pride—holier-than-thou hypocrites of a sad countenance appearing unto men to fast. Satan is clever: if he cannot lure the believer into Sodom with Lot he takes him to the other extreme and gets him into "a shew of wisdom in will-worship, and humility, and neglecting of the body" which only satisfies the flesh. Such poor souls frown on all wholesome and normal pleasures and receive him that is weak in the faith to doubtful disputations. They also are rebels against God's perfect will, also arguing, "Not so, Lord."

Much as we need separation from Sodom, we dread almost as much this overseparated brother who leans over backward. It is usually easier to convert a man out of Sodom than out of self-righteousness. The prodigal son is not so hard a case as the brother who stayed at home. Our Lord could win publicans and sinners, but of the Pharisees He said, "Let them alone." Peter was no Pharisee, he was honest, and God led him into the light, but in this day of grace we err as greatly as Lot when we argue in legalistic overseparation, "Not so, Lord." In either case, we are rebels against the perfect will of God.

17 ANOTHER CHANCE

AND the word of the Lord came unto the second time." Jonah missed his first chance, failed the Lord miserably, and suffered aplenty. But God did not disown him, He started him off again with new orders, all the wiser for a sad experience.

A little girl carrying a bottle of milk across the street fell down and broke the bottle. A neighbor shouted, "Now your mother will spank you!" "Oh, no," replied the little girl, "my mother gives me another chance."

Sometimes the Lord does spank us. He chastised Jonah. But He does give us another chance, not a chance to be saved after death, but a chance to serve Him afresh after we have failed.

It is a dreadful thing to be a castaway, a vessel the Master cannot use. In a Bible conference in Minnesota some years ago we had a piano that wouldn't stay tuned. We could not use it and finally had to push it over in a corner, where it stood in the dust, disapproved. Then we brought in another piano, which looked no better and sounded no better, except that it would stay in tune and, therefore, was approved.

I have seen ministers, Christian workers, set aside like the piano. They looked all right and were gifted, but they were out of tune. And I have seen others put in their places not half so gifted, by no means as impressive in appearance, but in tune.

And yet there is no reason why any of us should stand in the comer disapproved. We can be timed again!

"Down in the human heart, crushed by the tempter,

> Feelings lie buried that grace can restore;
>
> Touched by His loving hand, wakened by kindness,
>
> Chords that were broken will vibrate once more."

If you have failed God and He has put you in a corner, He does not expect you to stay there and whimper the rest of your life away. He gets no pleasure out of chastising you. He is ready to offer you another chance when you learn your lesson.

I think of Simon Peter after that fishing trip, which he described by saying, "We have toiled all the night and have taken nothing." Any expedition that starts with a human "we" ends with a humiliating "nothing." Then came the draught of fishes, and Peter fell at Jesus' knees, saying, "Depart from me; for I am a sinful man, O Lord." But did the Lord depart and give up Peter as a failure? Rather, He said, "Fear not; from henceforth thou shalt catch men." He offered him a greater chance!

And after a far more dismal failure than this, when Peter denied his Lord, there was another chance awaiting his repentance. Peter preaching with power at Pentecost is a preacher on his second chance! Some of the greatest stories in the annals of preaching are those of Jonahs to whom the word of the Lord came a second time.

You never please the devil more than when you sit around lugubriously because yon have failed. Repent and confess you must, but mere regret and remorse never honor God. God wants a broken heart, but a broken heart is more than a miserable heart. Esau repented after a fashion and so did Judas, but it was not the repentance of a second chance. A broken heart is not simply miserable; it is a heart broken to the will of God. There are miserable hearts aplenty still stubbornly set on their own way.

Repent as Jonah did, as Peter did, and the word of the Lord will come to you a second time. There will be another chance!

18 PAULS PERSUASION

I PITY the inquiring soul that starts out today moving from book to book, from preacher to preacher, seeking the truth. Whether he wants to know how to be saved or what to do after he is saved, he is likely to end up more puzzled than ever, with loads of learned lumber in his head but unable to build anything from it.

I remember that when I was studying the deeper Christian life I gathered a number of treatises on the theme and settled down to learn the truth. But by the time I had looked at the subject through the spectacles of all those disagreeing expositors, I came out with my head full of phrases—"the victorious life," "the Spirit-filled life," "the surrendered life," "perfect love," "baptism of the Spirit," "two natures," "three natures," "eradication," "entire sanctification," "the rest of faith"—and was in serious danger of becoming the disciple of a phrase instead of a Person. Then I learned that Christ Jesus is made unto us sanctification (1 Cor. 1: 30) and that sanctification, strictly speaking, is not something but Some One.

What is true of sanctification is true of every other spiritual truth. If the sinner had to wait until he could understand one doctrine of the atonement, let alone get all the scholars together on the subject, he would die in his sins. But the simplest soul can behold one dying on a tree and find .life in a look at the Crucified One. God is too wise to make the truth into a doctrine or a principle or a philosophy. Then only a few could ever grasp it. The Word became flesh and lived and died and rose a Person, and whosoever comes to Him shall not be cast out.

By Him all things consist. The Bible is simply God's Word about Christ. Christian doctrine is simply systematized truth about Christ. Christian experience is Christ living within. Christian work and service is the outliving Christ. The deeper Christian life is just more of Christ. The most important thing about the Lord's return is Christ. The main attraction of heaven is "to be with Christ." Beware that you do not merely believe a phrase and miss the Person I

If you ask me what is my persuasion, I answer that I am of Paul's persuasion: "I know whom I have believed and am persuaded that he is able to keep that which I have committed unto him against that day" (2 Tim. 1: 12). I fail Him often, but I know that years ago God through Christ started something in my heart that He has never stopped. God is no quitter, and having begun a good work in me, He will perform it. I do not know yet all about WHAT I have believed, for I do not know all about WHOM I have believed, but I know Him.

Paul was also persuaded that nothing could separate him or us who believe from the love of God in Christ (Rom. 8: 38, 39). And he was a persuader: "We persuade men" (2 Cor. 5:11). Being persuaded, he persuaded others. If your message carries no conviction, perhaps it is because you don't really believe it yourself!

But Paul's message was always Christ. Never seek satisfaction in any doctrine about Jesus. Press through to Him and touch Him for yourself! And don't spend your time explaining theories about Christ. Present Him. Men are not drawn to a doctrine or a phrase with any lasting profit. The sad finish of many a sect bears ample testimony to that. Don't try to attach people to a phrase; get them joined to Christ through saving faith and they are His to stay!

19 "BLESSED DOWNCASTINGS"

DO these lines fall under the eyes of some wearied Christian, some embattled warrior sore beset? Disappointed, discouraged, despondent, defeated, you are, in bitterness of soul, almost ready to give up the fight? Frankly, you are puzzled. You have prayed and nothing seemed to happen. You have read of victorious Christians, glowing accounts of amazing deliverance, but for you the waters have not divided, you have seen no pillar of cloud or fire, you just keep plugging along. You still believe the promises are true, you don't blame the Lord, but—well, somehow, you just don't seem to get off to the right start or to make the right connection.

And you are alarmed at the depravity and deceitfulness of your own heart. You have been a Christian for a long time, you read your Bible and pray, and you honestly want to please God, and yet there come trooping into your mind the most damnable thoughts and suggestions, until you wonder whether you are one of those who profess to know God but who deny Him and are abominable and disobedient and unto every good work reprobate. Honestly, you are having more temptations and troubles and battles now than when you started. It looks more like backsliding than growth in grace.

Now, that was what puzzled Mr. Timorous in *Pilgrim's Progress*. "The further I go, the more dangers I meet with," he said to Christian as the explanation of why he was running the wrong way. And Alexander Whyte said of him: "If poor old Timorous had only known it, if he had only had some one beside him to remind him of it, the very thing that so fatally turned him back was the best proof possible that he was on the right and the only right way; aye, and fast coming, poor old castaway, to the very city he had at one time set out to seek."

Beloved, think it not strange concerning this fiery trial, but count it all joy when you fall into diverse testings. "They who fain would serve Him best are conscious most of wrong within." If you think something new has struck you, read David in the Psalms. Read the *Confessions* of Augustine. Read Bunyan and Samuel Rutherford and David Brainerd. If you have had a look into the depths of your heart and been shocked and dumfounded, thank God! It is almost a forgotten experience today. In this age, when too often the church is but a mutual congratulation society, when man is thought to need polish instead of pardon, when dainty little theories of "living like Jesus" supplant the old dynamite sermons on sin and grace, praise God if now and then some mortal gets a right view of inward depravity and cries, "Woe is me! for I am undone."

Oh, I know your pretty talk about Puritanical introspection. Surely it avails nothing merely to look within if then we do not look without. But a right view of sin will sicken a man of himself and drive him to Jesus as nothing else will. Today we treat symptoms and never get at the disease.

Take heart, my brother. If your sense of failure, your alarm at your inward state terrifies you, it is a mark that you are in a fair way toward victory. Fly to Jesus and abide in Him. There is more hope for you than for all the Pharisees who need no repentance. It is a sign that you are beginning to see sin as God sees it and, therefore, God is working in you, for the devil certainly will never assist you in that direction.

"Blessed downcastings that drive us to Thee, O Lord," said Spurgeon. Yea, blessed indeed!

20 SPRING NOTES

IT is springtime in the hills. First, there came the advance notices, green among the trees, red along the water courses. Pussy willows hanging out their banners. Fleecy clouds, lazily drifting. Mountains wrapped in tenderest haze. Pink peach and white plum blossoms. The voice of the dove in the land proclaiming winter's war at end. The rolling call of the flicker that always makes me glad I'm alive. The clear elegance of the cardinal's song, fresh timed for happy days.

I've been down by the bridge where the yellow-throat plays peek-a-boo in the undergrowth; drowsing under the trees, scarcely stirred by the zoom of passing bees, lulled by the sing-song vireo; perched on a log by the swamp to hear the clear, wild challenge of the water thrush; and, finally, strolling homeward, stopping now and then for choice bars of the wood thrush's serenade from his cathedral in the woods.

The mocking bird is going over his varied repertoire. The pine warbler, sprite of the evergreens, sounds his contented little chant, and the ovenbird shouts his "preacher" song. The crested flycatcher announces that he has arrived and the kingbird sails around looking for trouble. The black-and-white warbler circles the tree trunks with his wiry lisp, sounding like the opening and shutting of a pair of scissors. Brand-new butterflies abound in gaudy colors. The hooded warbler, little monk of the undergrowth, is back again, and the black-throated green warbler invites everybody, "Ah, see, listen to me."

The tender green of the poplars blends with the darker shades of oak and the passing winter brown. Blue patches of sky, flaming red of maples, the pink of honeysuckle, and white of dogwood, yellow daisies, and the violets—all make a setting in this sylvan sanctum fit for a king. Ever since I saw John Burroughs' "Slabsides" in the Catskills, I have wanted a cabin deep in the woods.

It is pleasant to sit on the porch at home after darkness has fallen and the day is done, to watch and hear the night life of nature. And here is real wild night life! What better thing can earth afford us than to rest in the tender moonlight and watch the silent sky, the candles of the stars, the hobo clouds that wander? I hear the cricket beside the porch, the whip-poor-will from over the hill, a lone hoot owl in the swamp. The fireflies are out with their lanterns. What a pageant every night, and free of charge to him who will look and listen!

I would not care to live where there is but one season, be it ever so delightful. Appreciation is sharpened by contrast. To have battled through winter's hard discipline whets one's appetite for spring's reward. The wood thrush might grow tire- some if he sang all the year.

In the spiritual world, God has wisely arranged life's seasons for the growing of character. If we were meant to be care-free loafers in a lotus land of indulgent ease, things might have been arranged differently. But we are here to make character, and a Christlike character requires just such a universe as this. Strange as are the combinations of circumstance, odd as the dealings of Providence sometimes seem, often so bewildering that we can make neither head nor tail of it, this is still the ideal world for its present purpose. Hereafter, when we who believe shall be completely like Him, a new world will be ours, adapted to that state. But for our present business this world is the place. Even here, all things work together for good to them that love the Lord, to the called according to His purpose. And His purpose in saving us is to conform us to the image of His

Son (Rom. 8: 29). We have studied the meaning of predestination more than we have realized its purpose!

His changing seasons are best, both in the world of flesh and in the world of spirit!

21 MY CROWD

SEVERAL years of an itinerant preaching ministry over this land have impressed me again and again with the similarity of these times to the days of Malachi. That faithful, fearless prophet lived in a time of national decay, and when he thundered against sin, the only response from a nonchalant generation was the oft-repeated "Wherein?" that shows up all through his book. They considered Malachi a well-meaning but overwrought alarmist, and their "Wherein?" was the counterpart in that day of our modern "O yeah?"

But even in that desolate and desperate time God had His crowd: "Then they that feared the Lord spake often one to another." There has never been an hour so dismal that God did not have His crowd. From the faithful few in Noah's day to this tragic day of world distress He has had His remnant. Elijah may sometimes think himself the lone survivor, but there are always others who have not bowed to Baal. Whether the Christians of the Roman catacombs or the Reformation saints, Christ has had His irreducible minimum who speak often one to another.

In this present hour of apostasy I like to look out my window wherever I may be staying in America and watch those who love the Lord assemble. Whether I am speaking in a mission or under a tent or tabernacle or in a church, there is a thrill in watching them, whether few or many, start appearing from here and there, attracted by a common love for a changeless Christ in a changing world. Oh, I know that they have faults aplenty; there is much to deplore even among the best of them. But it is that same bond that joins our hearts today that bound together the saints of long ago, and we know that we have passed from death unto life because we love the brethren. And when one comes in from a train trip or from jostling with this wretched world on the streets, and finds a group gathered around the Book, it is like getting back into one's own country and one's native tongue. And indeed it is just that, for "our citizenship is in heaven" and ours is the language of Zion.

All over this land and all around the globe God has His crowd. It is small, for few there be in any age who find the way of life. It is not to be identified merely with the church crowd, for thousands of that great aggregation are not enrolled in heaven. It is not any select sect or movement. It is that assembly of all who know the Lord in saving faith and who through the new birth are members of the family of God.

The other night I watched from my window my crowd gather out of the darkness for the evening meeting. Yonder came an old lady whom grace had brought through many dangers, toils, and snares and who was persuaded that grace would bring her home. Over across the street came a bustling young man. I doubted for a moment that he could be coming my way, but soon I saw the glint of a Bible under his arm and I knew he was in my crowd, for precious few are they who will be caught out in public with a Bible. It was like a family reunion, though I had never seen them before.

I thank God for them. All over America they are assembling. Sometimes in most unlikely places one runs across them. Often they are persecuted, ridiculed, nicknamed. Some of it they bring on themselves, for they need guidance and often miss the mark. But a common loyalty to the old Book and the old faith binds them, and it is a mark of the times that God has reserved to Himself, through all the strata of our modern life, rich and poor, learned and unlearned, among all churches and races and conditions of men, those who fear the Lord and speak often one to another. They are His crowd and my crowd, and I love them!

22 BELIEVE—DON'T STUDY ABOUT IT!

THE healthiest faith is that which calls least attention to itself. It is well known that the person with best nerves is the one least conscious of nerves. Sometimes I have wondered whether or not the abundance of books and articles and sermons and discussions about faith is not an unhealthy sign.

God's Word does indeed speak much of faith, but there faith has no value of itself; it merely links us with the Lord. Neither the quantity nor quality of our faith matters most, but its object. It is easy to examine our faith and take the pulse and temperature of our faith until we are morbidly concerned, which, of course, soon kills it altogether. The sooner we quit bothering about it and simply trust the Lord, the better for us. We ought to be occupied with Him. The lover who is forever figuring whether or not he is in love is sure to destroy whatever love he may have.

We are easily deceived in this matter. We often suppose that the greatest believers are the ones who make most fuss about it, are always studying about it, bemoaning their lack of faith or exulting in their abundance of it, analyzing it, praying about it, discussing it. The fact is, such conduct really reveals a sick faith, an academic instead of active faith, ever learning but never knowing the truth. That is why God has chosen the babes instead of the wise and prudent. Those who trust God most and best often say least about it; they even seem unenthusiastic and unresponsive about discussing it; they sometimes seem blunt to those who worry about faith instead of believing. Such souls have learned to shy away from these dear chronic mortals who go in for studying about faith just as they get interested in some other sewing-circle enthusiasm and never really believe.

Any father would be distressed if his child lived worrying about whether he loved his parents or not. It is the spontaneous, unstudied naturalness of such affection that makes it precious. One does not get it *by* taking study courses or attending lectures. The people who really got the blessings of the Lord when He was among us in the flesh were the plainest people. They had no time to go to Bible conferences, nor were they profound enough to *study* faith, analyze their feelings, and explore their minds. They simply believed Jesus, and that was all. The ones who missed His blessing were the smart folks who had to think it over awhile, like the rich young ruler.

The fable of the mother bear who told her cub, " Shut up and walk! " when he wanted to know which foot to put forward first is a perfect illustration of what we are driving at. Faith in Jesus doesn't wait until it understands; in that case it wouldn't be faith. It doesn't wait until it feels just right. Faith in Jesus is of no value at all in itself. If it is real, we hardly know we have it. We are conscious of Jesus, not of faith. If we are conscious of our faith, whether much or little, then we are simply living in a subjective circle, pinching ourselves to see whether we hurt. Real faith is objective, we are taken up with Christ.

A little faith will work wonders if it is faith in Christ and if our mind is on Him, not on our faith. Don't study much about faith. Get your eyes on Him. Be taken up with Him. Look at Him through the Word, commune with Him in prayer, occupy your thoughts with Him. Try it, and the atmosphere will clear up. And if it doesn't clear up, it won't matter much, for you will get interested *in Him instead of in the atmosphere, and when you are happy in Him December's as pleasant as May!

23 A LETTER TO DAD

DEAR DAD:

Among the treasures of bygone years there's a faded old letter you wrote to me when I was a puzzled country boy away at college. I answered it then, but tonight, across the span of years, I'd like to answer it again. A lot of water has run under the bridge since, with scratchy pen, you put down those words of counsel to help me on the straight and narrow way. You have long since gone and I know you need no letter, for you see quite clearly from heaven's grandstand what is ofttimes so foggy to us who still run the race. A letter from me can give you little information, but one from you could certainly throw light on many a subject!

But just the same, I'd like to thank you better than ever I did when you were here for what you did and what you were. I am so glad that you believed the authority in the home belonged to you and not to me. I remember that time when your little boy tried just once to talk out loud to another little boy at church and disturbed the service. You handled that well: I never talked out again! I thank you for reading the Bible at bedtime before the old fireplace and then on bended knee committing us all afresh to our Father in heaven. My knees grew tired sometimes, but you built a wall around my soul that the devil was never able to tear down. I know you never kept up with the styles, and that funny fur cap I wore off to boarding school lingers still in my recollections: but I never knew the difference then and I get a good laugh out of it now, so no harm was done. You didn't have a lot to sell in your grocery store, but you gave away a lot in helpful words and godly counsel: you cast your bread upon the waters and some of it is coming back still today.

I remember the times I overheard you praying in that little store, reminding God that you had given me to Him and asking Him to remember His Word to you in which He had caused you to hope. I think you got a little shaky about me a time or two: it looked as if I were going to miss the track in spite of everything, but God didn't let you down, for He never lets anyone down. I'm preaching that old-time religion that you always hoped I'd always preach and partly because my father's prayers have followed me. As I look back over the road I've come and see how near I came to leaving it, I know that something greater than myself had a hand in it all; yes, not something but Some One, for the God of my father had an understanding with you and His eye was on me.

I've thought a lot of how you used to meet me when I came home from my preaching trips. When the train rounded that curve at the depot I could always see you standing beside the little old Ford, in that old blue suit that never was pressed again from the day you bought it. It never seems right to round that curve and not see you there. But there are other curves ahead, and when I get home for good I don't know how close to the gate of glory you can stand, but I'm sure you'll be on hand. I have wondered what you'll look like, but I'm sure I'll know you. And there'll be plenty of time to catch up on the conversation that was interrupted years ago.

You always liked to sing, though neither of us was unusually gifted that way. I am sure you're in great trim now, after all these years of practice. I am anxious to get over there and try out my brand- new voice with you on "Amazing Grace, How Sweet the Sound." From the looks of things down here, it probably won't be long till Jesus comes. I'll see you in the morning!

24 OVERDOING AND UNDERDOING

MATTHEW HENRY wrote with true perception when he described Naaman after his healing as making two mistakes, one of overdoing and the other of underdoing.

First, he wanted to take back with him some of the earth of the country where he had received so great a blessing. It was hallowed ground and he wanted to use it in his devotions back home. Whether he wanted to make an altar of it or keep it as a souvenir, it was not a good move. It had a touch of idolatry in it, even though Naaman was now turned from idols to worship the true God. "The earth is the Lord's," and Naaman needed not to carry dirt from Israel to Syria.

Here is an instance of a common error among believers, undue veneration for places and circumstances connected with blessing. Even the brazen serpent became a liability (2 Kings 18: 4) by undue glorification. Sometimes the place of one's conversion becomes a shrine, the preacher or verse instrumental in some great spiritual experience may be exalted unwisely. We build tabernacles to house our great visions, and Bethel becomes more precious than El-Bethel, the place rather than the God of the place. God is greater than any place, circumstance, or experience. That "happy day that fixed my choice" is a great day indeed, but only because the choice is fixed on "Him, my Saviour and my God."

The young believer, fresh from a glorious dipping in Jordan, often overvalues incidentals. Of course, most of that usually passes away, and when not overdone is just as precious as saving a memento of any happy day. But we must not lose the traveler in the baggage and clutter up our interests with details. We can become so busy hauling holy dirt that we forget God.

Then Naaman turned about and showed up just as poorly in the opposite direction by underdoing the matter. He said to Elisha: "In this thing the Lord pardon thy servant, that when my master goeth into the house of Rimmon to worship there, and he leaneth on my hand, and I bow myself in the house of Rimmon: when I bow down myself in the house of Rimmon, the Lord pardon thy servant in this thing."

In other words, Naaman has a heathen boss and he is asking an indulgence to escort his lord to worship and bow when his lord bows. Otherwise, there might be trouble. This is an old story. Many a believer makes reservation of a known sin to keep peace in the office or in the family. The covenant with God is made with tongue in cheek and fingers crossed. We hear Naaman's request often in modern parlance: "When the boss gets the force together, I take a drink along with them, for I couldn't afford to be a wet blanket "My husband goes to the theatre and I go along to keep peace in the family and then he goes with me to church on Sunday "When the neighbors call and suggest cards, I play as a sort of concession to courtesy "When I am out fishing with the fellows and somebody tells a dirty joke, I laugh with them, for I don't want to be a kill-joy." So they go on, tied up at home, in business, in the lodge and club, with the world, fearing the Lord and serving their own gods (2 Kings 17: 33). But we are to obey God rather than men and shun the very appearance of evil, and he who persists in underdoing will find it his undoing.

That Elisha bade Naaman go in peace takes nothing from the force of our lesson. A lot of water has run under the bridge since those days, and in this enlightened day of grace we must beware of the twin perils, that we neither overdo nor underdo.

25 THE TWO "SUFFICIENTS"

SUFFICIENT unto the day is the evil thereof" (Matt. 6:34). In other words, every day has enough troubles of its own. Therefore, there is no sense in borrowing from tomorrow, crossing bridges before we come to them. This universe is so arranged that a generous supply of trouble has been provided for each day; but some of us are not satisfied with our portion and so we create and invent a surplus for fear the stock should run low.

When we are not satisfied with the troubles we have, sometimes the Lord literally "snows us under" with so much that we don't have time to worry about it all. That may be a great blessing, for it is possible to get so far behind with our worrying that we give it up entirely. I know a dear brother who had just such an experience: he was wearing himself to pieces in fearful fretting, until so much descended upon him that he decided he never could have time enough to give to each trouble its proper amount of worrying, so he threw all his worries away.

We are not trying to be funny: it makes sense.

Everybody knows that worrying does no good, but nobody ever quits worrying just because he knows that. It takes some stunning experience to jolt us and knock us loose and make us desperate so that we have to do something about it. Of course, some get panicky and commit suicide or go to pieces. But many a man traces his victory to the day when something had to be done and like Br'er Rabbit who climbed the tree because he was "'bleedged to climb," the troubled soul makes a life-or-death plunge of faith and finds deliverance. Says Browning in his *Paracelsus:* ^u Are there not two points in the adventure of a diver—one, when a beggar he prepares to plunge; one, when a prince he rises with the pearl? " Many a ragged soul has so plunged into the sea of God's grace and come up rich—but the difference between pauper and prince lies in the PLUNGE!

That brings us to our other "sufficient": "My grace is sufficient for thee" (2 Cor. 12: 9). There is only one adequate provision for human need, the boundless grace of God. Therefore, hide in it. Hide in it for forgiveness, pardon for a sinful past. Hide in it for keeping for a troubled present. Hide in it for security in an eternal future. Hide in it for health and wisdom and peace. Hide there for needs of the family, the office, the pocketbook.

For it is the guarantee of heaven: "My grace is sufficient for thee." "My GRACE"—look what it is! "My grace IS sufficient"—look when it is, not may be or shall be sufficient, but IS sufficient NO! "My grace is sufficient FOR THEE"—look for whom it is! Not a few select saints, but for us ordinary souls in the wear and tear of the here-and-now. True, it was spoken to Paul, but it is ours as well as his, for God knows no favorites.

And when was it spoken to Paul? In some rare mood of inner exaltation? No, on one of his darkest days, when he learned that his troublesome thorn in the flesh was there to stay. Are you also up against the same old thing today? You have prayed, but your thorn is still with you? Well, something else, Some One else, is with you too. Sufficient unto the day is its sorrow, but sufficient also is His grace. As thy days not only shall thy sorrows be but also thy strength.

26 THE ETIQUETTE OF LOVE

"Love . . . doth not behave itself unseemly"

—1 Cor. 13: 5.

DEAR brother in the Lord who has known the great and small pulpiteers of the land once remarked that it wouldn't do to know some of the "big shots" too well. It is, indeed, a bit depressing, after sitting entranced listening to a masterpiece of exposition that lifts one into the heavenlies, to come to earth with a thump and listen dumfounded to the same expositor raving about his mail not coming on time or grumbling about his hotel room. Oh, yes, we know the answers and we do realize from experience the toll that weariness takes from our dispositions. We know also that we must keep our eyes on the dear Lord and not upon His instruments of clay.

And yet we do have some reason to expect that a seasoned veteran who has delved for years in the treasures of the Word, especially if he lectures to us about the Promised Land, should bear the fruits of Canaan with him. We shall desire more readily to possess the land if those who advertise it show us some sample figs and pomegranates and grapes of Eschol. Fortunately, most of the brethren do recommend their lectures by their lives, but so frail are these frames of ours, so often is the spirit willing and the flesh weak, that we must watch and pray to remember that love doth not behave itself unseemly.

Sometimes one who has attained prominence in the work of the Lord seems to assume a special license to misbehave and lay it to "unique personality." What would wreck us smaller fry if we undertook it is passed over as a sort of accompaniment to fame. But surely such a rule can have no place among the children of God. Age and experience in the things of God do not accentuate our crudities, they remove them. The mark of real greatness in the spiritual world is Christlikeness and the passing years should find us decreasing and Christ increasing as we are transformed into His image from glory to glory.

I know that some celebrities mightily used and honored have cut funny capers and seemed to enjoy shocking the saints by their antics. But they were used in spite of such conduct and will suffer loss for the misuse of their prominence. Would that they might learn that we poor ordinary mortals are weary and sick of such clowning. We see and hear it all day long in this poor silly world. When we come to God's house, we long to see Jesus and are moved by the marks of His cross. Greatness does not excuse unseemly behavior, it only makes such misconduct more serious.

Of course, we do not mean humor and wholesome naturalness. God has made us diverse in personality, and nothing is more precious than the many hues and colors of human temperament when the Spirit shines through. Certainly there is no place for hypocrites of a sad countenance, appearing unto men to fast. But we do mean that sourness and crankiness and petulance and overbearing egotism which can follow a great Bible lecture with grumbling at the waitress in the dining room. Our Lord spent a lot of time eating and visiting with common folk to teach us that love is proven more by etiquette than by eloquence.

Love does not tear its shirt. So keep yours on.

27 FIGHTING THE STARS

"The stars in their courses fought against Sisera"

—Judges 5: 20.

SISERA tried it. And it didn't work. It never does. The man who dares to go against the will of God, the purposes of the Almighty, never arrives. "The mother of Sisera looked out at a window, and cried through the lattice, Why is his chariot so long in coming? why tarry the wheels of his chariots?" You see, he didn't get there.

Do these lines fall under the eye of some one who hasn't arrived? We do not mean earthly success, your name in the papers. But you have not blossomed out into what you were meant to be. You are frustrated, and maybe anxious parents wonder what is wrong. Friends who hoped for much shake their heads behind your back. Maybe your wife is puzzled. She knows you have ability, and there is much about you that is fine. But you just don't seem to find your place. You're playing a losing game. The stars in their courses are against you. And the chariot wheels tarry. You do not arrive.

Don't be offended. I don't mean that you are another Sisera all the way 'round. But one doesn't have to be a Canaanite to fight the stars. Any man who is living at cross-purposes with the will of God, whether he is fully aware of it or not, is in the same plight as was this defeated warrior. Heaven is arrayed against him and he cannot win. He will be a disappointment to God, to himself, and to those who love him most.

On the other hand, the life in line with God's purposes has the stars on its side. "And we know that all things work together for good to them that love God, to them who are the called according to his purpose." Consider the PROCESS of

His purpose: foreknowledge, predestination, calling, justification, glorification. Consider the PEOPLE of His purpose: them that love God. Consider the PROVIDENCE of His purpose: all things work together for good. Consider the PROTECTION of His purpose: nothing shall be able to separate us from the love of God in Christ Jesus our Lord.

Get into that blessed purpose by trusting Christ as Saviour, abiding in Him, obeying Him as Lord. After all, the purpose of the believer's life is simply Christ: "For to me to live is Christ." When it comes to details, remember that if you will to do His will you shall know, for that is as true of direction and details as of doctrine.

Then fare forth to battle knowing that the stars in their courses fight with and for you. You are on the winning side, and this is the victory that overcometh the world, even our faith.

But if you are a rebel, you might as well give up fighting the stars. They belong to Him for whom they sing together. You are bucking the universe and its God, and your chariot will never return. Jonah tried it and bought a ticket but missed his destination. Only the schedule that God maps out will He allow us to fill. He who hath begun a good work in you will complete it. When He begins He will also make an end. Get into His program and you will arrive.

28 "GOOD FOR NOTHING"

"Ye are the salt of the earth: but if the salt have lost his savour, wherewith shall it be salted? it is thenceforth good for nothing, but to be cast out, and to be trodden under foot of men "—Matt. 5: 13.

IT is, as usual, a simple figure of speech that our Lord uses to set forth some of the saline characteristics of the Christian. Salt is purifying. Elisha used salt to heal the waters. There is something antiseptic about the presence and influence of God's people. How often does the entrance of a Christian sweeten and freshen the atmosphere like a breath of clean air in a stuffy room! Here is the only social gospel taught in the Word, the purifying presence of God's people in this diseased old world.

Salt preserves from spoiling and putrefaction. The world would have been utterly unendurable long ago but for the salt of the saints. When Christ takes up His own, it will become evident at once that the presence of the Spirit in the church has saved from utter decay until the appointed time.

But salt also seasons, gives flavor and relish, and just here some of the saints turn out to be good for nothing. The besetting sin of our Christianity today, in private and public, is insipidity. There is no taste to most of it. Drop into the average midweek prayer meeting and no further word will be necessary. We need not be amazed that the world pays no heed and passes by. We seem to conspire with the devil to make the meeting as dull and flat as we know how, and anything that might suggest color, tone, zest, and relish is promptly suppressed. Of course, in desperation many have gone to the other extreme and imported swing bands and tap dancers to enliven the proceedings. But there is nothing else so rich and full of flavor as the grace of God, and only our spiritual poverty is to blame for our savorless living.

We are to have salt in ourselves (Mark 9: 50) and in our speech (Col. 4:6). There ought to be such a seasoning of grace in us that our personalities and our conversation would be rich and tasty. There is something wrong with an uninteresting Christian. The early church had something on the day of Pentecost that made the world gather, amazed and confounded. Today men pass by unimpressed. The average believer is so savorless that men tread his testimony under foot. They do not even respect it, for he is so world-conformed that there is only profession without possession. He is a castaway.

There is still a lot of sound doctrine among the saints and plenty of activity, but we do need to do something about our taste. We are getting to be rather flat, and there is nothing to smack the lips over. Salt without savor may still be dressed up attractively, packed in a nice box with a ribbon around it, but it just isn't salt and it will soon be found out.

Church suppers and moving pictures in the basement and pin-the-tail-on-the-donkey contests won't do it. We need a good old revival that will stir up the gift of God and restore the lost joy of salvation and uphold us afresh with His free Spirit. We need a new heart and a right spirit and the love of God shed abroad within us. Then will transgressors be taught God's ways and sinners be converted.

We must do something about our flavor. Else we are good for nothing but to be cast out and to be trodden under foot of men.

29 WHAT LACK I YET

"WHAT lack I yet?" asked the rich young ruler (Matt. 19: 20). Apparently he lacked nothing. I think he must have been an impressive, handsome young fellow with lots of money and splendid moral character. He was reverent and he had come to Jesus seemingly in dead earnest seeking eternal life. He had kept the commandments from his youth. Surely he had everything.

The fact is, however, he had nothing and lacked everything. "One thing thou lackest," said the Lord: "go, sell whatsoever thou hast, and give to the poor, and thou shalt have treasure in heaven: and come, follow me." That the young ruler would not do, and because he missed that, he missed it al. He was a far finer character than Bartimaeus and Zacchaeus and the Syrophenician woman and the publican in the temple; but they got their blessing and he missed his. They lacked everything and knew it.

Our Lord said to His disciples: "When I sent you without purse, and scrip, and shoes, lacked ye anything? And they said, Nothing" (Luke 22: 35). Now, doubtless, they appeared to lack everything. Traveling preachers without purse, scrip and shoes, even under the conditions of their times, they certainly did not look prosperous. Yet they lacked nothing. WE NEVER LACK WHEN WE GO FORTH AT HIS BIDDING. He had given them their "Go" (Matt. 10: 6, 7), and because they went, they lacked nothing. He told the young ruler to go and because he went not, he lacked everything.

Of the early Christians it was written: "Neither was there any among them that lacked" (Acts 4: 34). It is always so with their kind. How could it be otherwise when He has promised to supply all our need? He has given us all things with Christ and He offers us abundance of grace. The world may cynically inquire, "If the Lord would make windows in heaven, might this thing be?" (2 Kings 7:2) but we know that God has said, "Prove me now herewith, ... if I will not open you the windows of heaven" (Mai. 3: 10). There are windows in heaven and showers of blessing and we are not sentenced to dwell in a desert I

How this poor world gets its standards mixed! To your average bustling modem business man, the rich young ruler would rate "tops" and the wandering preachers without purse, scrip and shoes would not be given a lift on the road. But our Lord knew who lacked and what they lacked and why. The man who misses the will of God is a pauper, though he have great possessions: the man who goes when God says "Go" is a prince, though he have no purse, nor scrip nor shoes. It is better to be Lazarus and beg for a crumb of bread on earth than to be Dives and beg for a drop of water in hell.

The plight of the Laodiceans was doubly bad because they "had need of nothing." Wretched indeed is the man who knows not his need. Count yourself a beggar, whatever you think you own, if you have not renounced it for His cross. Count yourself rich, though you have no purse nor shoes, if you are on His errand.

Jesus loved the rich young ruler. He was loved but lacking! Jesus loves you, too, and knows your need and longs to fill it Become a fool that you may be wise, and poor that you may be rich! "The young lions do lack and suffer hunger: but they that seek the Lord shall not want any good thing."

"When I sent you, ... lacked ye anything? And they said, Nothing."

30 GOING HOME

THE other day I watched from a high hotel window in a great city the milling crowd below. What a lonesome, homesick lot such mortals are! Little groups on the corners scanning the scary newspaper headlines, unable to make any sense of it all. Some strolling pensively along, smitten with a plague of thought. Others hurrying about in much ado about nothing. Never was a generation so bewildered, never so much like sheep having no shepherd.

What ails man is that, he is away from home. His real home is God, and he is restless until he rests in Him. But he has gotten away from home and, sick with sin, he hides from the only One who can hide him. He is a fugitive and has been since Adam hid in the garden. Like Jonah, he rises to flee from God's presence and knows not that he can hide from God only in God. He hides not only himself but what he has. Achan hid the wedge of gold; the one-talent man hid his talent. One hid the bad, the other the good, but both came to judgment. "He that covereth his sins shall not prosper." All through the Bible man is hiding, until at last he calls for rocks and mountains to hide him from the face of Him that sitteth upon the throne and from the wrath of the Lamb.

But he hides in vain. "My sins are not hid from thee," said the Psalmist, and God said, "Mine eyes are upon all their ways, they are not hid from my face: neither is their iniquity hid from mine eyes" (Jer. 16: 17). "Can any hide himself in secret places that I shall not see him? saith the Lord. Do not I fill heaven and earth? saith the Lord." Men make lies their refuge and under falsehood hide themselves but the hail and waters of judgment shall sweep them away (Isa. 28: 15-17).

The tragedy of it all is, the very One from whom he hides is the only hiding place. "I flee unto thee to hide me "Thou art my hiding place"; "Thou shalt hide them in the secret of thy presence from the pride of man; thou shalt keep them secretly in a pavilion from the strife of tongues."

"Rock of Ages, deft for me;

Let me hide myself in Thee."

The Christian is homed in God. "Your life is hid with Christ in God." And there is nothing morbid in the desire of the believer to go home. Paul desired to depart and be with Christ. We are pilgrims and strangers here, we seek an enduring city, and never did we feel less at home here than today. I have never seen so many tired saints as now. They are not tired of the way but they are tired on the way, and I don't believe there ever were so many weary travelers who are willing to stay but wanting to go as now. In my preaching journeys I see it on the faces in pulpit and pew, the mark of heavenly citizenship, the secret hope that tonight may be the night when He shall come and we shall go.

This is no mood born of frustration, it is the healthy longing of the soul. I know that, as for myself, God has been good to me and given me the desires of my heart. I have salvation and health and work and guidance and friends and companionship and every need supplied. But I should be a queer Christian if in this wretched world I did not lift up my head and rejoice that it is better farther on, for my redemption draweth nigh. Then let us exhort one another, brethren, since we see the day approaching!

"Then, cheer, my brother, cheer,"

WE ARE HEADED FOR HOME!

CPSIA information can be obtained
at www.ICGtesting.com
Printed in the USA
LVHW09s1532170818
587293LV00001B/249/P